The Best Of
DEBBIE FRIEDMAN

MUSICAL SELECTIONS FROM:
And The Youth Shall See Visions, Ani Ma'amin,
If Not Now When?, Not By Might/Not By Power
Sing Unto God

🎵 TARA PUBLICATIONS

ISBN 0-933676-12-3

Printed in the United States of America

CONTENTS

FOREWORD

Debbie Friedman's name has become synonymous with modern day Jewish music. Her five recordings and cassettes and her first volume *Not By Might, Not By Power,* have achieved an ever growing popularity. Her melodies are distinguished by beautiful melodic lines, exhilarating rhythm, exquisite lyricism and easy singability. They appeal to the younger generation while still finding favor with those having been nurtured on the older traditional melodies of the Jewish repertoire. Her song *Im Tirtzu* is known world-wide while *L'dor Vador* has become a synagogue classic. *Dodi Li, Dodi Tzach V'adom, V'erastich Li,* and *Wedding Vows* have become standards at nuptial celebrations throughout the United States and other parts of the world.

Tara Publications, in its untiring efforts to bring the best in Jewish music to the public is delighted to present these 36 representative songs of a very talented composer in one compact edition

Velvel Pasternak
Tara Publications

DISCOGRAPHY

The selections listed below are available on
the following recordings and cassettes:

AM—ANI MAAMIN
YSV—AND THE YOUTH SHALL SEE VISIONS
NBM—NOT BY MIGHT, NOT BY POWER
SUG—SING UNTO GOD
IN—IF NOT NOW WHEN?

Ahavat Olam	**AM**	L'cha Dodi	**SUG**
And the Youth Shall See Visions	**YSV**	L'dor Vador	**NBM**
Ani Maamin	**AM**	Mi Chamocha	**SUG**
Arise My Love	**AM**	Not By Might, Not By Power	**NBM**
Barchu	**YSV**	Ose Shalom	**YSV**
Barchu	**IN**	Priestly Blessing	**IN**
B'tzet Yisrael	**YSV**	Shehecheyanu	**YSV**
Dodi Li	**AM**	Shir Hamaalot	**IN**
Dod Tzach V'adom	**AM**	Sh'ma, V'ahavta	**SUG**
Et Dodim	**AM**	Sh'ma—You Shall Love	**YSV**
Etz Chayim Hi	**NBM**	Sing Unto God	**SUG**
Hodu	**YSV**	S'u Sh'arim	**NBM**
Im En Ani Li	**IN**	V'erastich Li	**IN**
Im Tirtzu	**AM**	V'shamru	**AM**
Kaddish	**SUG**	Wedding Vows	**IN**
Kumi Lach	**IN**	You'll Never Catch The Wind	**IN**
Laugh At All My Dreams	**AM**		

KEY TO TRANSLITERATION

a	as in c*a*r
ai	as in s*i*gh
e	as in f*e*d
ë	as in th*e*y
i	as in p*i*n or m*e*
o	as in f*o*rm or b*oa*t
u	as in tr*u*e
'	as in *i*t
ch	as in Ba*ch*

IM TIRZU

Music by Debbie Friedman

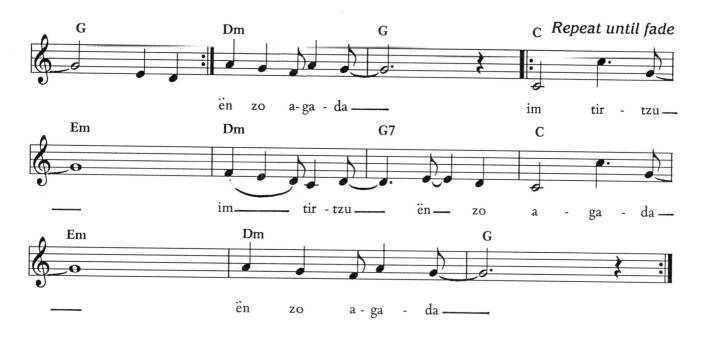

ën zo a-ga-da ____ im tir - tzu ____

____ im ____ tir - tzu ____ ën ____ zo a - ga - da ____

____ ën zo a - ga - da ____

אִם תִּרְצוּ אֵין זוֹ אַגָדָה
לִהְיוֹת עַם חָפְשִׁי בְּאַרְצֵנוּ
בְּאֶרֶץ צִיּוֹן יְרוּשָׁלַיִם

If you but will it—it is not a dream, to
be a free nation in our land, the land
of Zion and Jerusalem.

L'CHA DODI

Music by Debbie Friedman

Liturgy

Lively

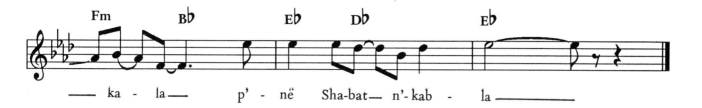

ka - la — p' - ně Sha-bat — n'-kab - la —

Come my friend to meet the bride
Let us welcome the Sabbath

לְכָה דוֹדִי לִקְרַאת כַּלָה
פְּנֵי שַׁבָּת נְקַבְּלָה

Liturgy

BARCHU

Music by Debbie Friedman

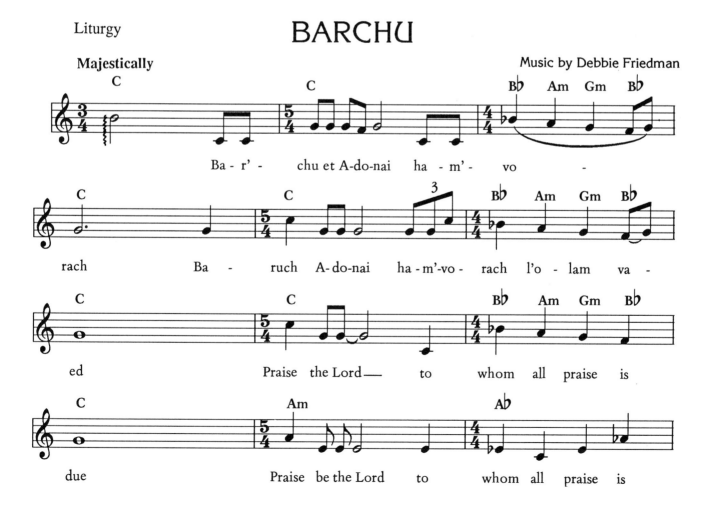

Ba - r' - chu et A-do-nai ha - m' - vo -

rach Ba - ruch A-do-nai ha -m'vo- rach l'o - lam va -

ed Praise the Lord — to whom all praise is

due Praise be the Lord to whom all praise is

בָּרְכוּ אֶת יְיָ הַמְבֹרָךְ
בָּרוּךְ יְיָ הַמְבֹרָךְ לְעוֹלָם וָעֶד

Praise the Lord to whom all praise is due
Now and forever praise the Lord

BARCHU

Liturgy

Music by Debbie Friedman

בָּרְכוּ אֶת יְיָ הַמְבֹרָךְ
בָּרוּךְ יְיָ הַמְבֹרָךְ לְעוֹלָם וָעֶד

Praised be the Blessed One
Blessed be Adonai
Praised be the Blessed One
Forever more

Liturgy

AHAVAT OLAM

Music by Debbie Friedman

Tenderly

te-cha l'-o-lam va-ed ki hëm cha-yë-nu v'-o-rech ya-më-nu u-va-hem ne-ge yo-mam va-lai-la ne-ge yo-mam va-lai-la v'-a-ha-vat-cha al ta-sir mi-me-nu l'-o-la-mim Ba-ruch a-ta A-do-nai o-hëv a-mo Yis-ra-ël o-hëv a-mo Yis-ra-ël

אַהֲבַת עוֹלָם בֵּית יִשְׂרָאֵל עַמְךָ אָהָבְתָּ
תּוֹרָה וּמִצְוֹת חֻקִּים וּמִשְׁפָּטִים אוֹתָנוּ
לִמַּדְתָּ עַל כֵּן יְיָ אֱלֹהֵינוּ בְּשָׁכְבֵנוּ וּבְקוּמֵנוּ
נָשִׂיחַ בְּחֻקֶּיךָ וְנִשְׂמַח בְּדִבְרֵי תוֹרָתֶךָ
וּבְמִצְוֹתֶיךָ לְעוֹלָם וָעֶד כִּי הֵם חַיֵּינוּ וְאֹרֶךְ
יָמֵינוּ וּבָהֶם נֶהְגֶּה יוֹמָם וָלַיְלָה וְאַהֲבָתְךָ
אַל תָּסִיר מִמֶּנּוּ לְעוֹלָמִים בָּרוּךְ אַתָּה
יְיָ אוֹהֵב עַמּוֹ יִשְׂרָאֵל

You have loved the house of Israel your people
With everlasting love. You have taught us Torah
and precepts, laws and judgments. May you
never take away your love from us. Blessed are
You, O Lord who loves your people Israel.

Liturgy

SH'MA – YOU SHALL LOVE

Music by Debbie Friedman

Tenderly

Sh'ma   Yis-ra - ël   A - do - nai_____ E-lo - hë - nu

A - do - nai   e - chad_____

Ba - ruch shëm   k' - vod_____ mal - chu - to

l' - o - lam va - ed_____

You shall   love the Lord your   God with all your   mind_____

_____ with all your   strength   with all your   be -

ing   Set these   words which I   com - mand   you this   day_____

_____ up - on_____   your_____ heart_____

—— I am the Lord your God ——————

שְׁמַע יִשְׂרָאֵל יְיָ אֱלֹהֵינוּ יְיָ אֶחָד
בָּרוּךְ שֵׁם כְּבוֹד מַלְכוּתוֹ לְעוֹלָם וָעֶד

You shall love the Lord your God
With all your mind, with all your strength
With all your being
Set these words which I command you this day
Upon your heart
Teach them faithfully to your children
Speak of them in your home and on your way
When you lie down when you rise up
Bind them as a sign upon your hand
Let them be a symbol before your eyes
Inscribe them on the doorpost of your house
And upon your gates
Ani Adonai Elohechem
I am the Lord your God

SH'MA, V'AHAVTA

Liturgy

Tenderly

Music by Debbie Friedman

Sh'- ma ———————— Yis - ra -

ël ———————————— A - do - nai ———————— E - lo -

hë - nu ———— A - do - nai ———————— A-do-nai e -

that ye may re-mem-ber and do all of my com-mand-ments
and be hol-y un-to your God
un-to your God un-to your God

שְׁמַע יִשְׂרָאֵל יְיָ אֱלֹהֵינוּ יְיָ אֶחָד
בָּרוּךְ שֵׁם כְּבוֹד מַלְכוּתוֹ לְעוֹלָם וָעֶד

And thou shalt love the Lord thy God with all thy heart
With all thy soul and with all of thy might
And all these words which I command you on this day
Shall be in thy heart that ye may remember
And do all of my commandments
And be holy unto your God

And thou shalt teach them diligently unto thy children
And thou shalt speak of them when thou sittest in thy house
When thou walkest by the way and when thou risest up
And when thou liest down and when thou liest down

And thou shalt bind them for a sign upon thy hand
And they shall be for frontlets between thine eyes
And thou shalt write them on the doorpost of thy house
And upon thy gates and upon thy gates

MI CHAMOCHA

Liturgy

Music by Debbie Friedman

Who is like you, O Lord among the mighty?
Who is like you, glorious in holiness, awe-
inspiring in renown, doing wonders?

מִי כָמְכָה בָּאֵלִים יְיָ מִי כָּמְכָה נֶאְדָּר
בַּקֹדֶשׁ נוֹרָא תְהִלֹת עֹשֵׂה פֶלֶא

V'SHAMRU

Liturgy

Music by Debbie Friedman

The children of Israel shall keep the Sabbath, observing the Sabbath through their generations as an everlasting covenant. It is a sign between me and the children of Israel forever.

וְשָׁמְרוּ בְנֵי יִשְׂרָאֵל אֶת הַשַׁבָּת לַעֲשׂוֹת
אֶת הַשַׁבָּת לְדֹרֹתָם בְּרִית עוֹלָם כֵּינִי
וּבֵין בְּנֵי יִשְׂרָאֵל אוֹת הִיא לְעוֹלָם

Liturgy

OSE SHALOM
ROUND

Music by Debbie Friedman

Slowly, gradually getting faster

May he who makes peace in the high places
Make peace for Israel and for all mankind
And say Amen.

עֹשֶׂה שָׁלוֹם בִּמְרוֹמָיו
הוּא יַעֲשֶׂה שָׁלוֹם עָלֵינוּ
וְעַל כָּל יִשְׂרָאֵל וְאִמְרוּ אָמֵן

Liturgy

KADDISH

Music by Debbie Friedman

With affirmation

24

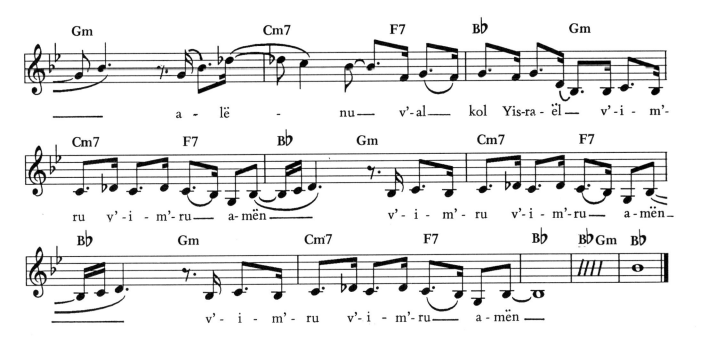

_____ a - lë - nu ___ v'-al ___ kol Yis-ra - ël ___ v'-i - m'-

ru v'-i - m'-ru ___ a-mën ___ v'- i - m'- ru v'-i - m'-ru ___ a-mën ___

v'- i - m'- ru v'-i - m'-ru ___ a-mën ___

יִתְגַּדַּל וְיִתְקַדַּשׁ שְׁמֵהּ רַבָּה בְּעָלְמָא דִי בְרָא כִרְעוּתֵהּ
וְיַמְלִיךְ מַלְכוּתֵהּ בְּחַיֵּיכוֹן וּבְיוֹמֵיכוֹן וּבְחַיֵּי דְכָל בֵּית
יִשְׂרָאֵל בַּעֲגָלָא וּבִזְמַן קָרִיב וְאִמְרוּ אָמֵן
יְהֵא שְׁמֵהּ רַבָּא מְבָרַךְ לְעָלַם וּלְעָלְמֵי עָלְמַיָּא
יִתְבָּרַךְ וְיִשְׁתַּבַּח וְיִתְפָּאַר וְיִתְרוֹמַם וְיִתְנַשֵּׂא וְיִתְהַדָּר
וְיִתְעַלֶּה וְיִתְהַלָּל שְׁמֵהּ דְּקֻדְשָׁא בְּרִיךְ הוּא
לְעֵלָּא מִן כָּל בִּרְכָתָא וְשִׁירָתָא תֻּשְׁבְּחָתָא
וְנֶחֱמָתָא דַּאֲמִירָן בְּעָלְמָא וְאִמְרוּ אָמֵן

Glorified and sanctified be God's great name
throughout the world which he has created
according to his will. May he establish his
kingdom in your lifetime and during your
days and within the life of the entire house
of Israel, speedily and soon; and say Amen.
May his great name be blessed forever and
to all eternity.
Blessed and praised, glorified and exalted,
extolled and honored, adored and lauded
be the name of the Holy One, blessed be
he, beyond all the blessings and hymns,
praises and consolations that are ever
spoken in the world; and say, Amen.

S'U SH'ARIM

Liturgy

Music by Debbie Friedman

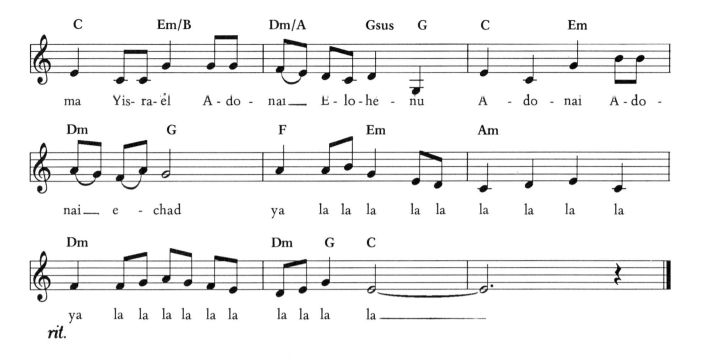

ma Yis-ra-el A-do-nai E-lo-he-nu A-do-nai A-do-

nai e-chad ya la la la la la la la la la

ya la la la la la la la la la la

rit.

שְׂאוּ שְׁעָרִים רָאשֵׁיכֶם
וְהִנָּשְׂאוּ פִּתְחֵי עוֹלָם
וְיָבֹא מֶלֶךְ הַכָּבוֹד
מִי זֶה מֶלֶךְ הַכָּבוֹד
יְיָ צְבָאוֹת הוּא מֶלֶךְ הַכָּבוֹד סֶלָה
הָבוּ גֹדֶל לֵאלֹהֵינוּ וּתְנוּ כָבוֹד לַתּוֹרָה
בָּרוּךְ שֶׁנָּתַן תּוֹרָה לְעַמּוֹ יִשְׂרָאֵל בִּקְדוּשָׁתוֹ
בֵּית יַעֲקֹב לְכוּ וְנֵלְכָה בְּאוֹר יְיָ
שְׁמַע יִשְׂרָאֵל יְיָ אֱלֹהֵינוּ יְיָ אֶחָד

ETZ CHAYIM HI

Liturgy

Music by Debbie Friedman

Ëtz cha - yim hi _____ ëtz cha - yim hi _____

ëtz cha - yim hi _____ la- ma-cha - zi - kim

ba _____ ëtz cha-yim hi _____ la -

ma - cha - la - ma-cha-zi - kim ba v' - tom-che - ha _____

_____ m' - u - shar

D' - ra - che - ha _____ dar - chë no - am _____

_____ v' - chol n' - ti - vo-te - ha

sha - lom ëtz cha - yim hi _____

last time to Coda
D.S. Coda

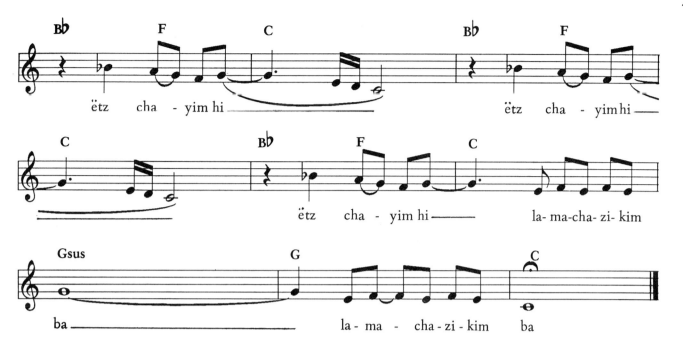

ëtz cha - yim hi _____ ëtz cha - yim hi _____

ëtz cha - yim hi _____ la- ma-cha- zi- kim

ba _____ la - ma - cha - zi - kim ba

עֵץ חַיִּים הִיא לַמַּחֲזִיקִים בָּה
וְתֹמְכֶיהָ מְאֻשָּׁר
דְּרָכֶיהָ דַרְכֵי נֹעַם
וְכָל נְתִיבוֹתֶיהָ שָׁלוֹם

It is a tree of life to those who take hold of it,
and happy are those who support it. Its ways
are ways of pleasantness, and all its paths are
peace.

Liturgy

PRIESTLY BLESSING

Music by Debbie Friedman

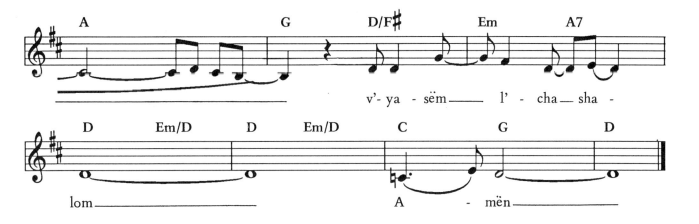

v'- ya - sëm___ l' - cha _ sha -
lom_____   A - mën___

May the Lord bless you and protect you;
May the Lord shine his countenance on you
And be gracious unto you;
May the Lord favor you and grant you peace.

יְבָרֶכְךָ יְיָ וְיִשְׁמְרֶךָ
יָאֵר יְיָ פָּנָיו אֵלֶיךָ וִיחֻנֶּךָ
יִשָּׂא יְיָ פָּנָיו אֵלֶיךָ
וְיָשֵׂם לְךָ שָׁלוֹם

L'DOR VADOR

Liturgy

Music by Debbie Friedman

33

Through all generations we will declare your greatness
To all eternity we will proclaim your holiness
Your praise shall never depart from our mouth

לְדוֹר וָדוֹר נַגִּיד גָּדְלֶךָ
וּלְנֵצַח נְצָחִים קְדֻשָּׁתְךָ נַקְדִּישׁ
וְשִׁבְחֲךָ אֱלֹהֵינוּ מִפִּינוּ לֹא יָמוּשׁ לְעוֹלָם וָעֶד

SHIR HAMA'ALOT

Liturgy
Joyfully

Music by Debbie Friedman

36

When the Lord turned again the captivity of Zion
we were like those who dream. Then our mouth
filled with laughter and our tongue with exultation;
then they said among the nations: The Lord has
done great things for them. The Lord has done great
things for us; we rejoiced.

שִׁיר הַמַּעֲלוֹת
בְּשׁוּב יהוה אֶת שִׁיבַת צִיּוֹן הָיִינוּ כְּחוֹלְמִים
אָז יִמָּלֵא שְׂחוֹק פִּינוּ וּלְשׁוֹנֵנוּ רִנָּה אָז יֹאמְרוּ
בַגּוֹיִם הִגְדִּיל יהוה לַעֲשׂוֹת עִם אֵלֶּה הִגְדִּיל
יהוה לַעֲשׂוֹת עִמָּנוּ הָיִינוּ שְׂמֵחִים שׁוּבָה יהוה
אֶת שְׁבִיתֵנוּ כַּאֲפִיקִים בַּנֶּגֶב הַזֹּרְעִים בְּדִמְעָה
בְּרִנָּה יִקְצֹרוּ הָלוֹךְ יֵלֵךְ וּבָכֹה נֹשֵׂא מֶשֶׁךְ הַזָּרַע
בֹּא יָבֹא בְרִנָּה נֹשֵׂא אֲלֻמֹּתָיו

Liturgy

B'TZET YISRAEL

Music by Debbie Friedman

38

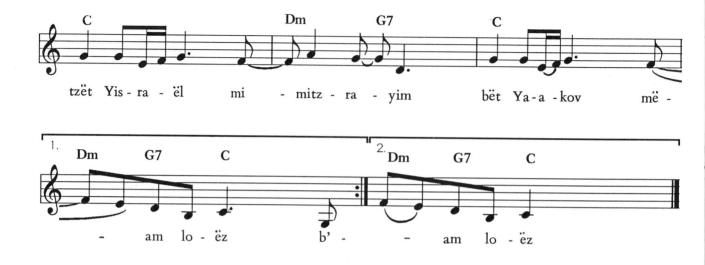

tzët Yis - ra - ël   mi - mitz - ra - yim   bët Ya - a - kov   më -

1.   - am lo - ëz   b' -   2.   - am lo - ëz

בְּצֵאת יִשְׂרָאֵל מִמִּצְרָיִם בֵּית יַעֲקֹב מֵעַם לֹעֵז
הָיְתָה יְהוּדָה לְקָדְשׁוֹ יִשְׂרָאֵל מַמְשְׁלוֹתָיו
הַיָּם רָאָה וַיָּנֹס הַיַּרְדֵּן יִסֹּב לְאָחוֹר

When Israel went out of Egypt, the house of Jacob from a
people of strange language; Judah became God's sanctuary,
Israel his dominion. The sea saw it and fled. The Jordan
turned back.

Liturgy

HODU

Slowly with intention

Music by Debbie Friedman

Give thanks to the Lord, for he is good;
His mercy endures forever.
Let Israel say: His mercy ....
Let the house of Aaron say: His mercy ....
Let those who revere the Lord say: His mercy ....

הוֹדוּ לַיי כִּי טוֹב כִּי לְעוֹלָם חַסְדּוֹ
יֹאמַר נָא יִשְׂרָאֵל כִּי לְעוֹלָם חַסְדּוֹ
יֹאמְרוּ נָא בֵית אַהֲרֹן כִּי לְעוֹלָם חַסְדּוֹ
יֹאמְרוּ נָא יִרְאֵי יי כִּי לְעוֹלָם חַסְדּוֹ

Liturgy

SHEHECHEYANU*

Music by Debbie Friedman

Deliberately

42

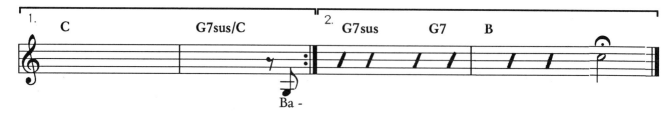

*Parts I and II can be sung together

בָּרוּךְ אַתָּה יְיָ אֱלֹהֵינוּ מֶלֶךְ הָעוֹלָם שֶׁהֶחֱיָנוּ וְקִיְּמָנוּ
וְהִגִּיעָנוּ לַזְּמַן הַזֶּה

Today we stand before you
To confirm our faith in the Holy One
To God for giving us life, for sustaining us
For enabling us to reach this season Amen

ANI MAAMIN

Liturgy

With conviction

Music by Debbie Friedman

44

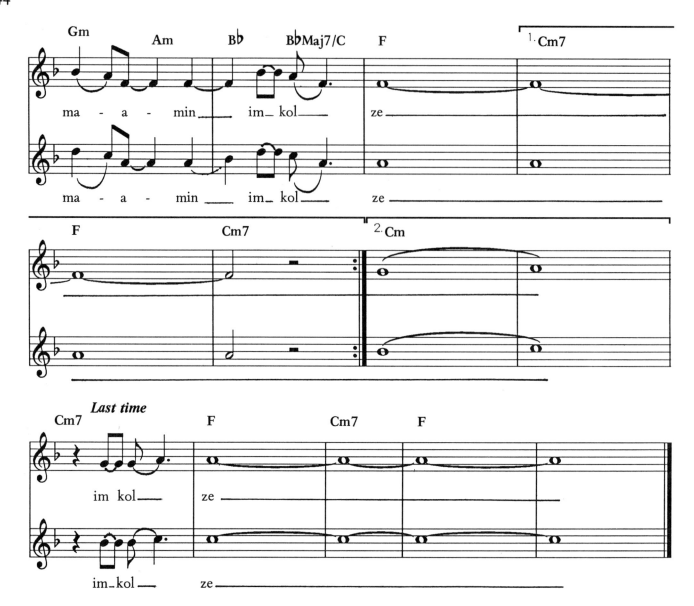

אֲנִי מַאֲמִין בֶּאֱמוּנָה שְׁלֵמָה בְּבִיאַת הַמָּשִׁיחַ
וְאַף עַל פִּי שֶׁיִּתְמַהְמֵהַּ עִם כָּל זֶה אֲנִי מַאֲמִין

I believe with perfect faith in the coming of the Messiah
and although he marry tarry I believe with perfect faith.

IM EN ANI LI/B'CHOL DOR VADOR

Ethics of the Fathers;
Haggadah Liturgy

Music by Debbie Friedman

46

If I am not for myself who will be for me?
If I am only for myself—what am I?
And if not now, when?

In every generation
one must look upon himself
as if he personally had come out of Egypt.

אִם אֵין אֲנִי לִי מִי לִי
וּכְשֶׁאֲנִי לְעַצְמִי מָה אֲנִי
וְאִם לֹא עַכְשָׁו אֵימָתַי

בְּכָל דּוֹר וָדוֹר
חַיָּב אָדָם לִרְאוֹת אֶת עַצְמוֹ
כְּאִילוּ הוּא יָצָא מִמִּצְרַיִם

KUMI LACH

Song of Songs

Music by Debbie Friedman

קוּמִי לָךְ רַעְיָתִי יָפָתִי קוּמִי לָךְ
כִּי הִנֵּה הַסְּתָו עָבַר
הַגֶּשֶׁם חָלַף הָלַךְ לוֹ

Rise, my love, my beauty, come away.
For lo the winter is over,
The rain is past and gone.

DODI LI

Song of Songs

Allegro

Music by Debbie Friedman

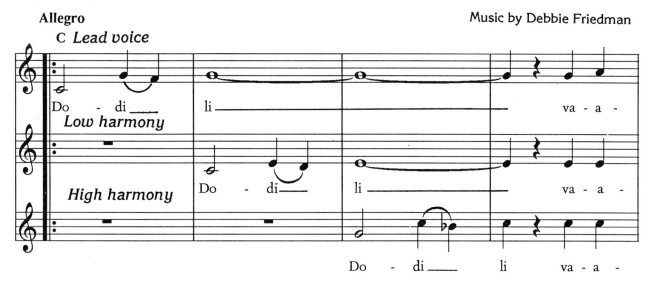

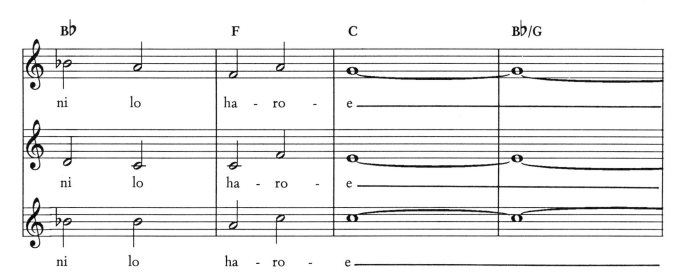

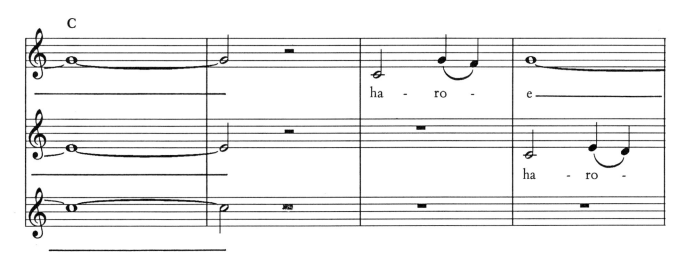

50

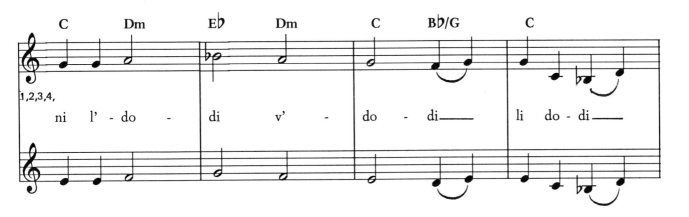

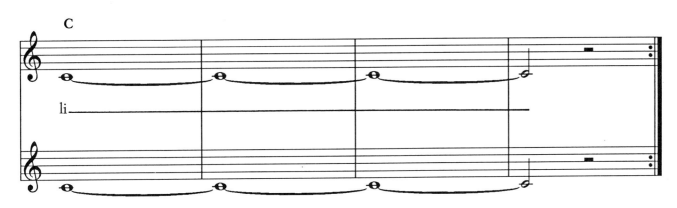

דּוֹדִי לִי וַאֲנִי לוֹ הָרוֹעֶה בַּשּׁוֹשַׁנִּים

א מִי זֹאת עוֹלָה מִן הַמִּדְבָּר
מִי זֹאת עוֹלָה
מְקֻטֶּרֶת מוֹר וּלְבוֹנָה   דּוֹדִי לִי

ב עוּרִי צָפוֹן וּבוֹאִי תֵימָן
וּבוֹאִי תֵימָן   דּוֹדִי לִי

ג לִבַּבְתִּנִי אֲחוֹתִי כַלָּה
לִבַּבְתִּנִי כַלָּה   דּוֹדִי לִי

ד אֲנִי לְדוֹדִי וְדוֹדִי לִי   דּוֹדִי לִי

My beloved is mine and I am his that feedeth among the lilies

Who is this coming up from the wilderness?
Who is this, perfumed with myrrh and frankincense?

You have ravished my heart, my sister my bride,
You have ravished my heart.

Awake, northwind, and come southwind
And come southwind.

ET DODIM KALA

Song of Songs

Music by Debbie Friedman

Ët do - dim ka - la _____

Bo - i l' - ga - ni _____

pa - r' - cha ha - ge - fen hë - në - tzu ri - mo - nim

ët do - dim ___ ka - la _____

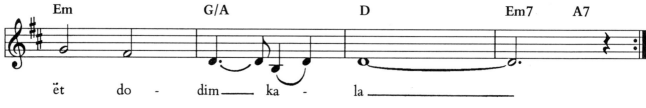

1. Kol do - di ___ hi në ze ___ ba

2. Ha - sh'mi - i - ni et ko - lëch

m' - da - lëg al he - ha - rim _____

ki ___ ko - lëch ___ a - rëv _____

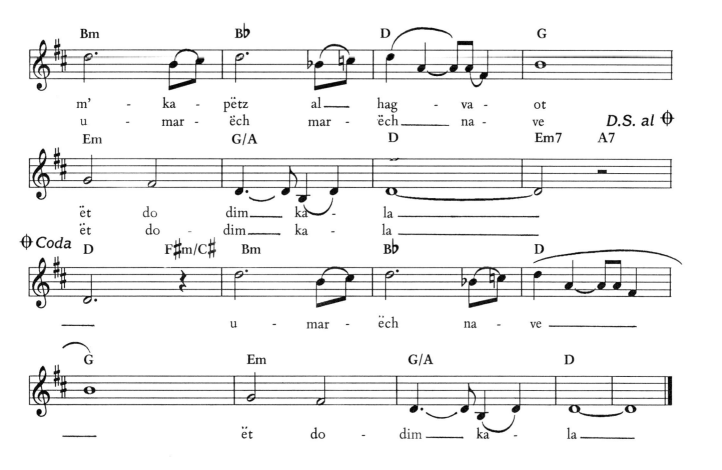

עֵת דּוֹדִים כַּלָּה בּוֹאִי לְגַנִּי
פָּרְחָה הַגֶּפֶן הֵנֵצוּ רִמּוֹנִים
קוֹל דּוֹדִי קוֹל דּוֹדִי
קוֹל דּוֹדִי הִנֵּה זֶה בָּא
מְדַלֵּג עַל הֶהָרִים
מְקַפֵּץ עַל הַגְּבָעוֹת
הַשְׁמִיעִנִי אֶת קוֹלֵךְ
כִּי קוֹלֵךְ עָרֵב וּמַרְאֵיךְ נָאוֶה

V'ERASTICH LI

Liturgy

Music by Debbie Friedman

I will betroth you to myself forever;
I will betroth you to myself in righteousness and in justice,
In kindness and in mercy.
I will betroth you to myself in faithfulness.

וְאֵרַשְׂתִּיךְ לִי לְעוֹלָם
וְאֵרַשְׂתִּיךְ לִי בְּצֶדֶק וּבְמִשְׁפָּט
וּבְחֶסֶד וּבְרַחֲמִים
וְאֵרַשְׂתִּיךְ לִי בֶּאֱמוּנָה

DODI TZACH V'ADOM

Song of Songs

Gently

Music by Debbie Friedman

Dazzling and ruddy is my beloved,
distinguished among ten thousand.
His head is fine gold, his locks are
curled.

דּוֹדִי צַח וְאָדוֹם דָּגוּל מֵרְבָבָה
רֹאשׁוֹ כֶּתֶם פָּז קְוֻצּוֹתָיו וְתַלְתַּלִּים

WEDDING VOWS

Wedding Liturgy

Moderately with feeling

Music by Debbie Friedman

Ba - ruch a - ta A - do -
nai _____ m' - ka - dësh a - mo Yis - ra - ël
al y' - dë chu - pa v' - ki - du - shin

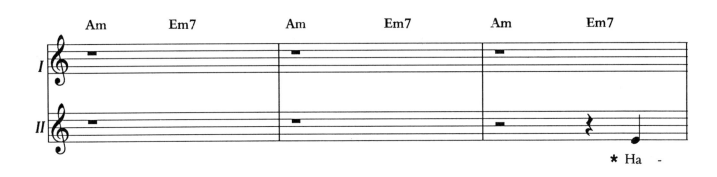

*Ha -

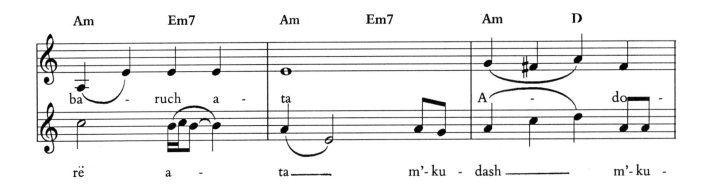

ba - ruch a - ta _____ m' - ku - dash _____ m' - ku -
rë a - ta _____ m' - ku - dash _____ m' - ku -

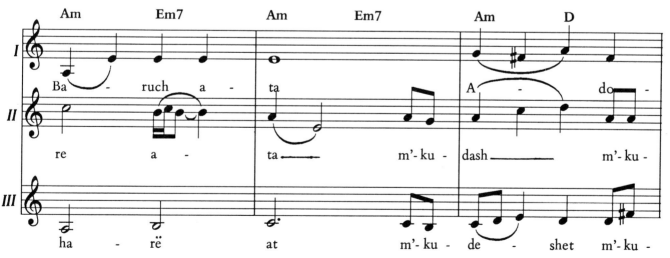

58

Blessed are you, O Lord, who sanctifies his people through *chupa* (the nuptials) and *kiddushin* (the betrothal)

Behold you are sanctified to me with this ring in accordance with the law of Moses and Israel.

בָּרוּךְ אַתָּה יְיָ מְקַדֵּשׁ עַמּוֹ יִשְׂרָאֵל
עַל יְדֵי חֻפָּה וְקִדּוּשִׁין

הֲרֵי אַתְּ מְקֻדֶּשֶׁת לִי בְּטַבַּעַת זוֹ
כְּדַת מֹשֶׁה וְיִשְׂרָאֵל

*הֲרֵי אַתָּה מְקֻדָּשׁ לִי בְּטַבַּעַת זוֹ
כְּדַת מֹשֶׁה וְיִשְׂרָאֵל

*Reform ritual

ARISE MY LOVE

Gently

Music by Debbie Friedman

Rise up my love my fair one_____ and come a - way_____ For lo the win-ter's passed_____ and the rain is_____ gone_____ The flow-ers ap - pear on earth_____ the time of sing-ing is come_____ and the voice of the tur - tle_____ is heard_____ The fig tree bring-eth forth_____

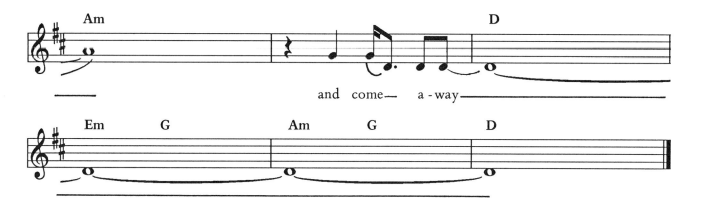

and come a-way

Rise up my love my fair one and come away
For lo the winter's passed and the rain is gone
The flowers appear on earth the time of singing is come
And the voice of the turtle is heard
The fig tree bringeth forth her green figs
And the vines in blossom bring forth their fragrance
Arise arise my love my fair one come away
Arise my love my fair one come away
Rise up my love my fair one and come away
Rise up my love my fair one and come away

SING UNTO GOD

Music by Debbie Friedman

Sing unto God sing a new song
O sing praises to God
Give thanks to God with a song
O sing praises unto the Lord thy God
Rejoice in the Lord all ye righteous
And cry out to the Lord with joy
Sing out from your hearts O sing praises to God
Bless God's name O sing unto the Lord a song of praise
Sing praises to the Lord sing unto God
Sing a new song unto God

NOT BY MIGHT, NOT BY POWER

With strength

Music by Debbie Friedman

Not by might and not by power
But by spirit alone shall we all live in peace
The children sing, the children dream
And their tears may fall
But we'll hear them call and another song will rise
Not by might not by power shalom

YOU'LL NEVER CATCH THE WIND

Music by Debbie Friedman

Gently

To all of you lit-tle ones— I sing this song for you for your life a-head is pre-cious— and your mo-ments are so few I'll tell you a sto - ry— though you may not un - der - stand of a man who spent his life - time hav-ing vis - ions— run-ning cir - cles— chas - ing— wind

67

To all of you little ones I sing this song
For you for your life ahead is precious
And your moments are so few
I'll tell you a story though you may not understand
Of a man who spent his lifetime
Having visions running circles chasing wind
Once upon a time I spent my life
In a restless search for the truth
Running after rainbows reaching for the clouds
I know I was chasing the wind
And so to my little ones my dreams are now for you
May the rainbows you run after be the rainbows inside of you
And as for the clouds let them fly away and be they are ours
But for the moment 'cause you'll never no you'll never catch the wind

LAUGH AT ALL MY DREAMS

Gently

Music by Debbie Friedman

70

Laugh at all my dreams my dearest laugh and repeat anew
That I still believe in people as I still believe in you
By the passion of our spirit shall our ancient bonds be shed
Let the soul be given freedom let the body have its bread
For my soul is not yet sold to the golden calf of scorn
For I still believe in people and the spirit in them born
Life and love and srtrength and action in our hearts and blood shall beat
And our hopes shall be both heaven and the earth beneath our feet
Laugh at all my dreams my dearest laugh and repeat anew
That I still believe in people as I still believe in you

AND THE YOUTH SHALL SEE VISIONS

Music by Debbie Friedman

Very rubato

Verse 1

Child-hood was for fan - ta - sies — and nurs-'ry rhymes and toys — The

world was much too bus-y —— to un-der- stand small girls and boys — As

I grew up — I came —— to learn that life —— was not a game —— that

her-oes just were peo - ple that — we called an-oth - er name — And the

72

Childhood was for fantasies for nursery rhymes and toys
The world was much too busy to understand small girls and boys
As I grew up I came to learn that life was not a game
That heroes just were people that we called another name

And the old shall dream dreams and the youth shall see visions
And our hopes will rise to the sky
We must live for today, we must build for tomorrow
Give us time, give us strength, give us life

Now I'm grown the years have passed I've come to understand
There are choices to be made and my life's at my command
I cannot have a future 'til I embrace the past
I promise to pursue the challenge time is going fast
And the Today's the day I take my stand
The future's mine to hold
Commitments that I make today are dreams of days of old
I have to make the way for generations come and go
I'll have to teach them what I've learned so they will come to know

That the old shall dream dreams and the youth shall see visions
And our hopes will rise to the sky
We must live for today, we must build for tomorrow
Give us time, give us strength, give us life

KADDISH D'RABANAN

Music by Debbie Friedman

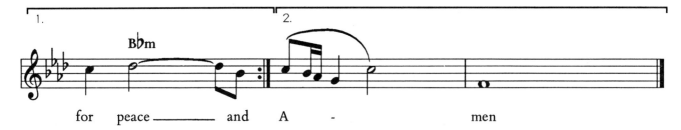

for   peace ———— and   A -   men

*Kaddish D'rabanan (Scholar's Kaddish) is recited after the reading of talmudic or midrashic passages. The end section, **Al Yisrael V'al Rabanan** (the basis for this composition) is a prayer for the welfare of the scholars.*

For our teachers and their students
And the students of their students:
We ask for peace and loving kindness
And let us say Amen
And for those who study Torah
Here and everywhere may they be blessed
with all they need and let us say Amen
We ask for peace and loving kindness
And let us say Amen.

L'CHI LACH

Music by Debbie Friedman

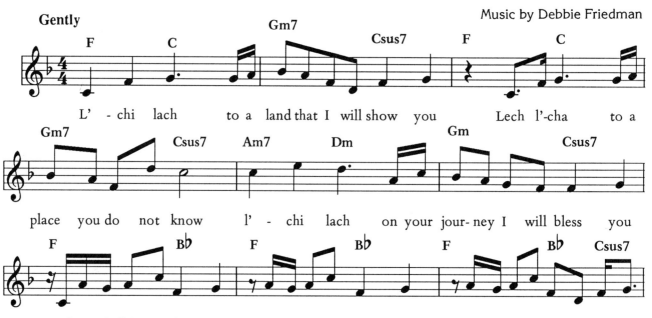

L' - chi lach   to a land that I will show you   Lech l'-cha   to a

place you do   not know   l' - chi lach   on your jour- ney I will bless   you

and you shall be a bless- ing   you shall be a bless - ing   you shall be a bless-ing l' - chi

lach

L' - chi lach and I shall make your name great

lech l'- cha and all shall praise your name l' - chi lach to the

place that I will show you l'- sim-chat choch- ma l'- sim- chat choch- ma
cha - yim cha - yim

l' - sim-chat choch-ma l' - chi lach and you shall be a bless- ing

you shall be a bless - ing you shall be a bless-ing l' - chi lach

L'chi lach to a land that I will show you
Lech l'cha to a place you do not know
L'chi lach on your journey I will bless you
And you shall be a blessing you shall be a blessing
You shall be a blessing l'chi lach
L'chi lach and I shall make your name great
Lech l'cha and all shall praise your name
L'chi lach to the place that I will show you
L'simchat chochma [l'simchat chayim] l'chi lach
And you shall be a blessing l'chi lach

B'RUCHOT HABA'OT

Music by Debbie Friedman

B'ruchot haba'ot tachat kanfe hash'china
B'ruchot haba'im tachat kanfe hash'china
May you be bless'd beneath the wings of the *sh'china*
Be bless'd with love, be bless'd with peace.

ALEF BET

Music by Debbie Friedman

Aleph, Bet, Vet, Gimel, Dalet, Hë,
Vav, Zayin, Chet, Tet, Yud, Kaf,
Chaf, Lamed, Mem, Nun, Samech,
Ayin, Pë, Fë, Tzadi, Koof, Resh,
Shin, Sin, Taf

This is an "Echo" song. Soloist sings each bar which is repeated by group.